An Intimate Note to the Sincere Seeker

SRI SRI
RAVI SHANKAR

VOLUME 6: July 27, 2000 – July 8, 2001

ART OF LIVING FOUNDATION

An Intimate Note to the Sincere Seeker;
Weekly Knowledge from Sri Sri Ravi Shankar
VOLUME 6: July 27, 2000 – July 8, 2001

Published by
Art of Living Foundation
Post Office Box 50003
Santa Barbara, California 93150
(877) 399-1008 (U.S. toll free)
(805) 564-1002
Printed in the United States of America

ISBN 1-885289-40-5

Compiled by Bill Hayden and Anne Elixhauser
Cover Design and Art Work: Bill Herman
Editorial Review: Laura Weinberg

When a river meets the ocean, the river no longer remains a river. It becomes the ocean.

A drop of the ocean is part of the ocean.

In the same way, the moment a devotee meets or surrenders to the Divine, the devotee becomes God.

When the river meets the ocean, it recognizes that it is the ocean from the beginning to the end.

Similarly, the individual "I…. I…." dissolves in one Divinity.

- Sri Sri Ravi Shankar

OTHER WORKS BY THE AUTHOR

Wisdom for the New Millennium
God Loves Fun
Waves of Beauty
Bang on the Door

Talks published singly:

The Language of the Heart
Prayer, the Call of the Soul
The Way Back Home

The teachings of Sri Sri Ravi Shankar are available in
the form of books, video recordings and audiotapes.

For a catalog of products and to order, contact:
Art of Living Bookstore
(877) 477-4774 U.S.A. or (641) 472-9892
Fax: (641) 472-0671
E-mail: bookstore@artofliving.org

An Intimate Note to the Sincere Seeker

*Here in your hands is
the sixth treasure book
of intimate notes from*
Sri Sri Ravi Shankar
-a gift of love to cherish.

Introduction

In June of 1995, Sri Sri Ravi Shankar began a weekly tradition of creating a short talk on a subject that was relevant to current events or to the collective minds of those who walked his path. Not only does the current Weekly Knowledge - as we call these intimate notes - apply to an immediate issue or need, but there have been many instances when someone seeking wisdom or advice, picked up a volume and randomly opened it to find exactly what was needed at that moment. The paradigm of time, space and separateness breaks down.

Those who are lucky enough to be with Sri Sri when the knowledge is created, find that the discussion brings forth truths that satisfy the heart and enrich the intellect. It is always lively, extemporaneous and creative. In the words of Sri Sri, "Being with the guru means spontaneous integration of life and wisdom."

Included with each Weekly Knowledge is a News Flash that documents the journey that Sri Sri takes around the world and through people's hearts and lives. In the News Flash, Sri Sri is called Guruji, the name many have chosen to call him out of respect and love.

These talks have been collected each year into volumes and made available to the whole world. The journey for this collection begins on July 27, 2000 at the European Ashram in Germany and ends at the Guru Purnima Course on July 8, 2001 at Lake Tahoe, California, United States.

Table of Contents

ACTION AND REACTION

*A*ction comes out of conscious decision. Reaction comes out of impulsiveness. Impulsiveness creates a chain of karma. Reaction and non-action both create karma, but conscious action transcends karma. Although conscious action does not create new karma, non-action can. For example, a soldier in war and a policeman using tear gas do not create karma, but a doctor who does not give medicine to a patient in need incurs karma.

Through knowledge and devotion, transcend all karma and be free.

News Flash
The Youth Training Program at the Bangalore Ashram is in progress with 150 participants from southern India. Meditation sessions are being conducted in the Indian Pavilion at the international Expo 2000 in Hanover, Germany. The European Ashram is bustling with activity and joy. A sudden thundershower had ecstatic devotees giggling and running down the slopes along with our mischievous master!

Jai Guru Dev

TECHNOLOGY

*T*he purpose of technology is to harness nature to bring information and comfort to human beings. When spiritual values - human values - are ignored and neglected, instead of bringing comfort, technology brings fear and destruction.

Technology without human values considers nature a dead object. Science gives insight into the life of nature, and spirituality makes nature come alive. In the eyes of children there is nothing dead in the world - animals, trees, the sun and the moon - they all have life, they all have emotions, they all have feelings. But in the eyes of a stressed and ignorant person, even human beings are like robots - objects!

Technology without spirituality is destructive. Spirituality is the technology of consciousness, and the whole world is the play and display of consciousness.

News Flash
The first Art of Living Course was held in Kosovo.

The Bangalore Ashram has 250 enthusiasts in teacher training.

Every inch of the European Ashram is filled with smiling faces.

Guruji was welcomed with much fanfare at the Indian Pavilion at Expo 2000 in Hanover, Germany with the traditional Aarti and a Manipuri dance. From there he walked through the Avenue of Trees, with devotees sprinkling rose petals in his path, and then to the Christ Pavilion where he was welcomed by African drummers. Accompanied by the melodious strains of a harp, he held a powerful meditation and spoke on the theme of the Expo: Humankind-Nature-Technology. The depth of silence was felt even in the prayer service, which ended with Guruji being taken ceremoniously to sign in at the special gallery - the glass facade of the church!

Jai Guru Dev

LOVE - THE QUESTION OF AN ANSWER

*I*n a congregation, Sri Sri asked, "How many of you feel strong?" Many people raised their hands.

Sri Sri then asked, "Why?"

"Because you are with us," they answered.

"Only those who feel weak can surrender," Sri Sri responded.

All those who were feeling strong were taken aback; they suddenly felt weak!

If you are in love, you feel weak because love makes you weak. Yet there is no power stronger than love. Love is strength. Yet love is the greatest power on earth. You feel absolutely powerful when you are with the Divine.

Someone asked: But why do we keep alternating between strength and weakness?

Sri Sri: That is the fluctuation in life.
When you feel weak - surrender.
When you feel strong - do seva.

News Flash
This News Flash cannot contain all the reports from the 1,500 villages adopted by the 5H Program (Health, Homes, Hygiene, Human Values and Harmony in Diversity) in India. In New Delhi, Guruji was busy appreciating all the good work, attending to problems, consoling grievances and correcting lapses.

Jai Guru Dev

CONFLICT AND INNOCENCE

*F*ights can only happen among equals. When you fight with someone, you make that person equal. But in reality there is no one at par with you. When you keep people either above or below you, then there is no fight.

When people are above you, you respect them. When they are below you, you love them and you feel compassionate. Either submission or compassion can take you out of a fight in no time. This is one way to look at a situation when you are tired of fighting. But when you are well rested, just fight and have fun.

The same is true of the mind. When the mind is caught up in the senses or thinks it is equal to the senses, there is constant conflict. But when the mind is smaller than the senses, as in animals, there is no conflict. And when it realizes that it is bigger than the senses, there is no conflict. When the mind transcends the senses, it comes back to its true nature, which is innocence - "in no sense."

Does this make sense? *(laughter)*

News Flash
Malawi, in central Africa, became the newest country to join the Art of Living family.

The jubilant Teacher Training Course and about 100 youth leaders have completed their training programs and will be serving 1,000 additional villages in the southern states of India for the 5H Program.

The Discovery Channel discovered the bliss in the ashram.

Jai Guru Dev

PROBLEMS? ONE MORE

The first solution to a problem is not to have the problem at all. *(laughter)*

The second solution is to willingly accept the problem and see it as a challenge.

The third solution is to know that the problem is a boogey man; it is not real.

The fourth solution is to know that nature has provided you the solution even before giving you the problem. First you met me and then you had a problem. *(laughter)* When it snows, there are no bacteria since herbs to heal you do not grow in that season. In the spring, the herbs come first and then the bugs. In the summer, the shade comes before the summer sun gets strong. So, nature takes good care of you.

Sabya: What if longing is a problem?

Sri Sri: Longing ripens you. Do not solve all your problems. Keep at least one of them. You need something to munch on - and life goes on.

News Flash
Another 100 youths moved on to 5H projects in Andhra
Pradesh, Karnataka and Tamil Nadu in a moving
graduation. Guruji met with the Shankaracharya of
Kanchi before flying to Bombay where a satsang, which
was supposed to be quiet and secret, included 4,000 people.

Krishna's birthday was celebrated in the European Ashram.

Jai Guru Dev

DO NOT MAKE A MISTAKE BY POINTING OUT MISTAKES

A lady came to Sri Sri and said that her husband lied to her. She was very upset. Sri Sri asked, "Why does your husband lie to you? He lies to you because he loves you, and is afraid to lose your love or to hurt you. If he did not love you, he wouldn't lie to you."

Do not tell a person a mistake he knows that he made. What is the use of pointing out a mistake that he knows he has committed? By doing this, you will only make that person feel more guilty, defensive or resentful and this will only create more distance.

You should only point out the mistake of a person who does not know, but who wants to know. Also do not point out the mistake of a person who knows but does not want you to know about it. Often people know the mistakes that they have committed, but they do not want you to tell them.

Think about the usefulness of your comments. Before pointing out a person's mistake, see whether your comments in any way will help to improve the situation, foster love or bring harmony. A magnanimous person does not pick on the mistakes of others and make them feel guilty. Instead, they correct other's mistakes with compassion and care, not through words but through their attitude.

∽

News Flash
Washington, D.C. had big satsangs and a lovely boat ride with Guruji. The D.C. Mayor's office honored Guruji by proclaiming that henceforth August 26th would be celebrated as His Holiness Sri Sri Ravi Shankar Day. Senator Paul Strauss presented this honor to Guruji at the elegant ball room of the Capitol Hilton in the presence of 1,500 people.

In the United Nations in New York City, Guruji's speech was by far the best, and he was given a standing ovation. Among other wonderful things, he talked about how spirituality was the fruit of the banana and religion was the banana peel. At the end of the talk, people were asking each other, "Are you the banana, or are you the peel?" One person was heard commenting, "I am the monkey, I get both the banana and the peel!"

Jai Guru Dev

WISE ARE THE ONES WHO MAKE YOU CRAVE FOR THE DIVINE

*U*nfortunate are those who crave for the world.
Fortunate are those who crave for the Divine.
Unwise are those who make you crave for the world.
Wise are those who make you crave for the Divine.

The source of conflict is the notion of "mine" and "yours." Self-knowledge eases the sense of limited belongingness and resolves this conflict.

When knowledge dawns in you, there is no stranger in the whole world! At the same time you realize that you know very little about even the nearest one.

Suchak: Yes, our nearest one often remains a stranger.

Sri Sri: You cannot understand anyone totally, for life is a mystery!

Marcy: But Guruji, you understand us totally! *(laughter)*

Sri Sri: Wake up and see. All these distinctions, "Me, mine, others," simply dissolve.

News Flash

During the United Nations Millennium World Peace Summit in New York, the elders of the last of the Incas of Peru spotted Guruji and recognized him as The Man Of Light. They bestowed their highest honor upon him to the sounds of their ancient conches and flutes.

At the Montreal Ashram, Katherine called and "complained" that Guruji would not leave her digital camera. Each time she downloaded the pictures and tried to erase them from the camera, one particular picture of Guruji always remained in the camera!

After the "mini" Advanced Course over the Labor Day weekend, Guruji gave informal talks to packed halls in Montreal and Ottawa.

Sixteen fortunate devotees rose in Divine Love with the master - in a hot-air balloon! When they were asked how they had felt being "in space" with him, they gleefully replied, "Absolutely at home!"

Jai Guru Dev

Do You Have to be Thankful and Feel Obliged?

*W*hen you are on a spiritual path, you are not thankful or obliged to anybody. In the Gita, Krishna says, "He is dear to Me who neither goes on thanking people nor hates anyone (Na abhinandati na dveshthi)."

Thanking and feeling obliged indicates that you believe in someone else's existence rather than in the Divine who rules everything. When you feel obliged, then you are not honoring the principles of karma or the Divine Plan.

Appreciate people for what they are; do not thank them for what they do. Otherwise your thankfulness is centered around ego. Be grateful, but do not be grateful for an act. Be grateful for what is. As every individual is nothing but a puppet of the ONE, thanking and being obliged is simply an exhibition of ignorance. Everything is ruled, controlled and managed by one Divinity. That consciousness has to shine forth in every act of yours; you do not need to make a mood of it.

Question: Guruji, we are so grateful to you, what should we do?

Sri Sri: When you have a total sense of belonging, then gratefulness does not become an obligation. Such gratefulness is for the Divine only, and this gratefulness enhances your strength.

∽

News Flash

Guruji addressed members of the Indian Association at Staten Island, N.Y. along with the Prime Minister of India. He also graced the Ayurvedic Conference and enlivened the discussion by giving Ayurveda a spiritual dimension that was otherwise hidden.

Many solutions for the tourism industry emerged when Guruji delivered his wisdom at the Confederation of Indian Industry at Agra, India. At dawn, the minarets of the Taj Mahal seemed to bow in reverence welcoming Guruji and his entourage. Despite Guruji's repeated instruction to look at the Taj Mahal, the devotees' attention remained focused on him.

Jai Guru Dev

DIVINE LOVE AND THE COMPLAINING FACE

*H*ow would you like to see yourself - happy and bubbling with enthusiasm, or dull and difficult to please?

Sometimes you like to be pleased, appeased and cajoled, so you put on a tough, upset face and act difficult to please. If a person has to appease and please ten people all the time, it is so tiring. People who keep a long face and expect others to cajole and appease them, make others run away. Lovers often do this. They expend a lot of energy in cajoling and this reduces the joy and celebration of the moment.

It is okay for you to show your upset mood or tendency once in awhile, but doing it repeatedly is taxing for you and the people you love.

If you feel down, appease and please yourself. Your need to be appeased by someone else is a sign of grossness. This is the root of ignorance. If you want attention, all you get is tension.

Become one whose enthusiasm never dies, come what may.

It is not possible to attain Divine Love with a complaining face. The complaining face is a sign of an unaware mind. If you want to complain, complain to God or your guru because both have their ears covered. *(laughter)*

∞

News Flash
From a village near Alwar in Rajasthan, India, a nine-year-old girl, Uma, who was dumb from birth started speaking after her ART Excel Course. The same was reported of a twelve-year-old boy from Vallabh Vidyanagar in Gujarat.

Talakatora Stadium in Delhi was aptly decorated for a grand satsang. Thousands who could not enter the stadium could still fully participate thanks to the big screens provided by the organizers. Guruji went to Rishikesh to inspire and to get inspired by the 108 youth leaders who were beginning their service work for the 5H Program.

Jai Guru Dev

THE DEVOTEE BECOMES GOD

*W*hen a river meets the ocean, the river no longer remains a river. It becomes the ocean. A drop of the ocean is part of the ocean. In the same way, the moment a devotee meets or surrenders to the Divine, the devotee becomes God. When the river meets the ocean, it recognizes that it is the ocean from the beginning to the end. Similarly, the individual "I.... I...." dissolves in one Divinity.

Question: What about backwaters?

Sri Sri: Sometimes the ocean goes into the river to greet it. Sometimes it seems that the ocean is pushing back the river. Similarly, the Divine puts many questions and doubts in the mind or provides an amazing experience to bring you back home.

News Flash
Construction activities for the meditation hall, the water tank and more residential facilities are in full swing at the Bangalore Ashram to enable more devotees to participate in future celebrations.

Jai Guru Dev

DEVOTION IS STEEPED IN MYSTERY

One who is not amazed by the magnificence of this creation - his eyes are not yet opened. Once your eyes are opened, they close and this is meditation. *(laughter)*

Tell me, what in this creation is not a mystery? Birth is a mystery; death is a mystery. If both birth and death are mysterious, then life is certainly a greater mystery, isn't it?

Being completely immersed in the mystery of life and this creation is samadhi.

Your knowing or believing does not really matter to what Is.

This creation is an unfathomable secret, and its mysteries only deepen. Getting steeped in mystery is devotion. The "Scene" is a mystery; the "Seer" is a mystery.

Deepening the mystery of Creation is science. Deepening the mystery of the Self is spirituality. They are the two sides of the same coin. If neither science nor spirituality can create wonder and devotion in you, then you are in deep slumber.

∞

When a materialistic person tells you a secret, it will only create doubts and spread malaise.

When a wise or spiritual person tells you a secret, it will uplift your consciousness and spread benevolence.

∞

News Flash
Every day poor people were fed at the Bangalore Ashram during the Navratri Celebration. More than 5,000 people in the slums were given clothes. Guruji has just emerged from his week-long silence looking more resplendent than ever. News about healing experiences continues to flood in from all over the world.

Jai Guru Dev

PERFECTION IS THE NATURE OF THE ENLIGHTENED

*I*n a state of ignorance, imperfection is natural and perfection is an effort.

In a state of wisdom or enlightenment, imperfection is an effort but perfection is a compulsion and is unavoidable.

Perfection is taking total responsibility, and total responsibility means knowing that you are the only responsible person in the whole world. When you think that others are responsible, then your degree of responsibility diminishes.

When you are in total Vairagya - dispassion - you take care of even trivial and insignificant things with such perfection. For example, during the puja every morning, Sri Sri decorates the puja table in flowers with such great care, choosing different color combinations and patterns every day, fully knowing that the decoration will not last even 10 minutes.

After the puja he himself removes the garlands from the puja table or showers people with flowers from it. Yet even while he is in a deep state of samadhi, he effortlessly and lovingly decorates the puja table every day. It is obvious that it does not matter how the flowers are arranged - attention to such a trivial thing with such keen awareness can only come through utter dispassion.

Perfection is the very nature of the enlightened one.

∽

News Flash
Celebration continues as always.

Jai Guru Dev

Ignorance of Your Capability Can Expand You

Always know that the Divine never gives you a responsibility you cannot fulfill. No one ever expects you to treat them if you are not a doctor. No one will ask you to fix their wiring system if you are not an electrician.

Your responsibility is only what you can do. And you do not know what you can do. Always accept that you do not know what you can do.

Ignorance of your capability can expand you.

When you know what you can do, you can progress. But when you do not know what you can do, you can grow by leaps and bounds.

When you know what you can do, you can do things. When you do not know what you can do, you can do things even better!

Jai Guru Dev

LOVE IS THE SHADOW OF THE SELF

When you love something, you have a sense of belongingness with it. You can only love something when it belongs to you. If it is not yours, you cannot love it. Love is the shadow of the Self.

The bigger the Self, the bigger the shadow, and the bigger the love. When love is cast over all of creation, then you are the Big Self. That is Lordship.

When Lordship dawns in the Self, there is perennial celebration.

∽

Today is Deepawali, the festival of lights. There are many stories associated with this day.

It was on this day that the demon Narakasura was killed. King Narakasura - Naraka means hell - had been granted a boon that he could only be destroyed by a woman. Lord Krishna's wife Satyabhama was the one to destroy him.

Why could only Satyabhama kill Naraka? Satya means truth and bhama means the beloved. Untruth or lack of love cannot conquer hell. It cannot be removed by aggression. Hell can only be erased by love and surrender. Non-aggression, love and surrender are the inherent qualities of a woman. Hence only Satyabhama, the true beloved, could remove hell and bring the light back. And Narakasura's last wish was that every house should celebrate his demise with lights to mark the end of darkness. This is Deepawali.

It was also today that Lord Rama returned to Ayodhya, his kingdom, after his victory over Ravana, the demon king. Ayodhya means that which cannot be destroyed, that is, life. Ram means the Atma - the Self. When Self rules in life, then knowledge lights up. There is life everywhere. But when the spirit is awakened in life, Deepawali happens.

❧

News Flash
Priyansh, a two-and-half-year-old boy, was playing with his friends on his eighth floor balcony. A while later his sister came running in shouting that her little brother had fallen from the balcony and was lying flat on the ground below. When everyone went down, his father thought that the boy was dead. To their surprise they found the child was blissfully lying down without even a tooth broken. Barring a small injury to his leg, everything was fine. When asked, Priyansh told his father that Guruji had saved him.

Jai Guru Dev

Are You a Tourist or a Pilgrim?

What is the difference between a tourist and a pilgrim?

Both are on a journey. Where a tourist satisfies the senses, a pilgrim is in a quest for truth. A tourist gets tired and tanned, while a pilgrim sparkles with spirit. Every move a pilgrim makes is done with sacredness and gratitude, while a tourist is often preoccupied and unaware.

A tourist compares his journey with other experiences and places and thus is not in the present moment. But a pilgrim has a sense of sacredness so he tends to be in the present moment.

Most people in life are just tourists without even being aware of it. Only a few make their life a pilgrimage. Tourists come, look around, take pictures in their minds, only to come back again. But pilgrims are at home everywhere - they are hollow and empty.

When you consider life as sacred, nature waits on you.

Are you a tourist or a pilgrim?

☙

News Flash
Diwali was celebrated in the Bangalore Ashram. With the Festival of Lights setting in, 50 people got back their sight, while thousands received insights. On the first anniversary of Amma's mahasamadhi, Guruji related the meaning of Amma's name, Visalakshi - "one with broad vision."

"Broad vision gives you your guru and in turn your guru gives you broader vision."

Guruji was a State guest in Orissa where he arrived after a brief satsang in Chennai. Though it was the first time in Orissa, the arrangements and the enthusiasm were simply unmatchable as Guruji mesmerized a crowd of more than 35,000 people. Guruji went to Jagannath Puri, the Eastern seat of wisdom, where Vishnu Yagna was performed. Puri had a great satsang, where many people reported miraculous healing experiences.

A report from Argentina tells us about the stunning experience of a medical team on the miraculous disappearance of a malignant tumor after their patient had been given 48 hours to live.

Jai Guru Dev

THE BODHI TREE

*B*uddha was enlightened under the bodhi tree. He then stood up and watched the tree from a distance for seven days. He took sixteen steps towards the tree and under each step blossomed a lotus flower. This is the legend.

The bodhi tree is symbolic of both sansara - the world - and dharma. The lotus flower symbolizes clarity, dispassion, love, beauty and purity.

It is only when you are detached in life that you can watch the sansara and all of its plays. When you witness the sansara, every step you take is benevolent and impeccable. When every action of yours is preceded by witnessing, then every move you make in this sansara becomes perfect and significant.

News Flash

Guruji's entourage moved to Jamshedpur where a crowd of more than 20,000 was enthralled by the master. Then on to Ranchi where another 60,000 were soaked in his grace. Later in the night, Guruji met with more than a thousand villagers who came just to have a glimpse of him.

The City of Joy - Calcutta - was full of enthusiasm. Guruji addressed the Confederation of Indian Industries. Guruji's program in Calcutta was three satsangs back to back over two days. Hundreds and thousands of people enjoyed the hospitality of West Bengal. Devotees were doubly stunned when an aggressive heckler was instantly transformed into a seeker who danced in joy.

Then Guruji moved on to Gaya to offer tribute to his most beloved mother, our Amma, on the first anniversary of her death. And once again the bodhi tree had another date with the enlightened.

Jai Guru Dev

NIMIT - INSTRUMENT OF THE DIVINE

*W*hen you are neither clear nor confused, only then can you be a perfect instrument of the Divine. How would an instrument know what is going to be, and when? How can an instrument be confused, and how can an instrument be clear?

This state is called Nimit - just being an instrument of the Divine. Being very clear means not opening up to new possibilities; this can lead to limitations. But unlimited possibilities are open to one who is neither clear nor confused.

Your mind swings from clarity to confusion and from confusion to clarity. But the state in which there is no doership and no inertia is the most creative and progressive state.

Sharmila: Will this not lead to lethargy?

Sri Sri: No. A sharp instrument does its job perfectly, effortlessly.

Sharmila: What about focus?

Sri Sri: Focus is natural to a dynamic consciousness.

Confusion arises when new information flows in and clarity is lost. Then confusion again seeks clarity. Clarity constricts the possibility of new information. A confused consciousness seeks clarity and every confusion breaks away from clarity.

If there is only confusion, there is frustration. If there is only clarity, there is rigidity.

After giving contradictory knowledge, Krishna tells Arjuna, "Just be Nimit!" And to be an instrument, the prerequisite is to be madly in love. That is why in love there is neither confusion nor clarity; or there are both confusion and clarity simultaneously.

Nazreen: Is truth more important than love?

Sri Sri: I'm confused! Is it clear? *(laughter)*

News Flash
Allahabad, the city of the Kumbha Mela, had thousands blissed out at its first satsang with the master.

Under the full moon, the meditation at the Sangam - the confluence of the main rivers - took the rowboats full of devotees beyond time - an amazingly mystical experience. High Court judges had the privilege of meeting with the master. Enthusiastic villagers greeted Guruji when he visited the 5H model villages.

Delhi bustled with activity - so many seva projects, so many meetings. Guruji also gave the keynote address at a U.N. program for promoting tolerance among religious leaders.

The performance of our school at Bangalore has startled educators - sixteen prizes and seven first prizes! An amazing record from a rural school of first generation literates competing against established institutions in the state.

Jai Guru Dev

THE PROBLEM'S SOLUTION

*W*henever there is a problem, we either deny it saying there is no problem or we sit to solve the problem and make it a big issue. Neither of these help. A problem does not disappear when you deny it. And it does not get solved when you sit to solve it. The five steps to solve a problem are:

✦ Acknowledge the problem - it is there.

✦ See it as a small problem, and do not say it is big.

✦ If it concerns people, keep in touch with them instead of avoiding them.

✦ Talk less and give time a chance.

✦ Get together and celebrate. When you celebrate and put the problem on the back burner, you will see that the problem gets solved in time.

So it is wise not to sit to solve a problem. Most of the meetings to solve problems end up in disaster.

If you do not have any problem, you will create problems for others! *(laughter)* If you have a small problem in your pocket to solve, it will give focus to your mind. If you do not have any problems, you may be a problem for others. It is better to have a problem than to be a problem.

News Flash
The south zone organizers of India who came to solve
problems finally found out that they had only one problem:
they had no problems.

In New Delhi, the Imam Maulana Illyasi, who is the
president of the organization of Imams in India met with
Guruji along with the Turkish delegation and participated
in a satsang. Back in Bangalore, Guruji gave the
concluding address at the Confederation of Indian Industry.

Before leaving for Frankfurt, Guruji made a brief stopover
at Chennai, where he spent the two hours there going into
the city to motivate the twenty-five 5H youth leaders, the
Yuvacharyas.

Jai Guru Dev

SACREDNESS AND YOU

*T*hroughout the ages, in all cultures, certain places, times, persons and symbols were considered sacred. The Native American Indians and the tribals in India consider the earth, sun, moon and all the directions to be sacred. In the ancient tradition, the Rishis considered all the rivers, mountains and even animals, trees and herbs to be sacred. And what of people? They are definitely sacred.

In different parts of the world, certain symbols, certain places and different times of the year are considered sacred. Various cultures honor certain people and consider them to be sacred. For Christians the cross, Jerusalem, Christmas and the Pope are sacred. For Muslims, the crescent moon, Mecca and the month of Ramadan are sacred. The Hindus consider the river Ganges, the Himalayas and the Swamis to be sacred.

When you consider a symbol, place, time, person or act sacred, your attention is undivided and whole. When things are ordinary and the same, you tend to slip into unawareness and inertia. The moment you consider something sacred, your inertia disappears and you become more alive. There is nothing as fulfilling as a sacred act. You put your heart and soul into a sacred act. When every action of yours becomes sacred, you have become one with the Divine. Then every minute of your life, every place you go, every act of yours is sacred and every person you meet is only your reflection.

Question: Why does an act when performed repeatedly lose it sacredness?

Sri Sri: This happens when your memory overpowers your consciousness and you lose your sensitivity. For example, people living in Benares do not feel that it is a sacred place. That sensitivity is just not there.

Question: How can we preserve that feeling of sacredness in our acts?

Sri Sri: Through living in the present moment and through sadhana. Your sadhana will not allow your memory to overpower consciousness. Then repetition is not a hindrance.

It is good to feel that some symbols, places, time and people are sacred so that you can be awake and alive. But eventually you need to transcend and feel that the entire creation and your whole life are sacred. For the man of God, the whole world, with all its symbols, places and people are sacred at all times.

Be a man of God!

News Flash
*Guruji was the star attraction and the public magnet at
the PSI Conference in Basel, Switzerland.*

*Guruji presented the Human Values Award 2000 to Max
van der Stoel, the OSCE (Organization for Security and
Cooperation in Europe) High Commissioner on national
minorities, at the International Association for Human
Values Conference in Amsterdam, Holland. The conference
was attended by several dignitaries including the former
prime minister of the Netherlands, who was one of the
keynote speakers. Guruji left an indelible mark in
Amsterdam. A well-organized satsang with many
intelligent questions and knowledge flowing from the
master left the packed hall spellbound and asking for more.*

*Guruji's entourage walked in no-man's land between
Germany and Switzerland!*

Jai Guru Dev

I am God

*I*t was thought that to say "I am God" is blasphemy. I tell you, to say "I am not God" is blasphemy. When you say, "I am not God," you deny God His omnipresence.

You are made up of love. If you say, "I am not God," you are denying that God is love. If you are love and you say, "I am not God," you are saying God is not love, and that is blasphemy.

"I am" is your consciousness. If you say, "I am not God," you deny that God is aware, alert and awake. You exist. When you say, "I am not God," you deny God a portion of existence, and that is blasphemy. You are denying the scriptures that say, "God made man in His own image." If you say, "I am not God," you are denying God.

Question: If God is omnipresent, why is there hatred and suffering in this world?

Sri Sri: Just as in a movie, it does not matter whether it is a tragedy or a comedy, or one with a happy ending; in the Absolute there are no opposites. All the opposites are part of relative existence.

38

Relative existence is not the complete picture. Good and bad, right and wrong, everything is relative. For example, milk is good, but too much milk can kill you. A drop of poison can save a life - most medicines have "Poison" written on them. These are neither absolutely good nor bad; they just are.

Truth transcends duality, and God is the absolute and only truth. In a movie, when light passes through the film, it does not matter to the light what the film is. Tragedy or comedy, hero or villain, the light is always there.

In the same way, no matter what is happening in your mind, you are God.

∞

News Flash
As soon as Guruji landed in Bombay there was a Mahakriya for 15,000 people followed by a satsang of 50,000!

Art of Living was the most "happening" thing in all of Northern Kerala. The largest grounds and stadiums in every city were brimming over with jubilant faces. In Thrissur, 1 lakh (100,000) people turned up for satsang, in spite of a "bandh" and a complete transportation strike! On to Palghat, where two lakh of devotees eagerly welcomed the master. Calicut, with over two lakh people, was next, and then came Kannur, a politically disturbed small town. All the different religious and political factions forgot their differences for a day, and sang united and strong in a satsang of over two lakh of people!

And then on to Mangalore for an intimate satsang.

Guruji visited five major cities in five days, and many other cities in 10-15 minute stopovers. Each of these places had enthusiastic satsangs with huge crowds. Nearly one million people in Kerala participated in satsang and meditation in the presence of the master in the last five days!

Jai Guru Dev

Atheism is Not a Reality

*I*t is difficult to see God as formless and it is difficult to see God as having a form. The formless is so abstract and God in a form appears to be too limited. So some people prefer to be atheists.

Atheism is not a reality; it is just a matter of convenience. When you have a spirit of inquiry or when you search for truth, atheism falls apart. With a spirit of inquiry, you cannot deny something that you have not disproved. An atheist denies God without first disproving God's existence. In order to disprove God, you must have enormous knowledge. And when you have enormous knowledge, you cannot disprove it! *(laughter)*

To say that something does not exist, you must know about the whole universe. So you can never be one hundred percent atheistic. An atheist is only a believer who is sleeping!

For a person to say, "I don't believe in anything," means he must believe in himself - so he believes in a self that he does not even know.

An atheist can never be sincere because sincerity needs depth - and an atheist refuses to go to his depth. The deeper he goes, he finds a void, a field of all possibilities and he has to accept that there are many secrets he does not know. He would then need to acknowledge his ignorance - which he refuses to do - because the moment he is sincere, he seriously starts doubting his atheism. A doubt-free atheist is next to impossible! So you can never be a sincere and doubt-free atheist.

When the atheist realizes his ignorance, what does he do? Where does he go? Does he go to a guru? What does a guru do to him? *(The answer next week.)*

News Flash
Guruji addressed a packed auditorium of prominent scientists and researchers at the Indian Institute of Sciences, Bangalore - the premier institute of India - where he praised the students for initiating a dialogue on "Bridging Science to Humanity." Dr. Abdul Kalam, scientific advisor to the Prime Minister, expressed immense admiration for Guruji.

Then Guruji left on a whirlwind trip to Vishakhapatnam where 10,000 children, who are a part of our 5H Program, received blessings.

Hyderabad had been promised a surprise visit which was a four-hour stop with only 24 hours notice. There were still hundreds queuing for darshan at Guruji's departure.

The 109th country to become a part of the Art of Living map is Mozambique, Africa.

Jai Guru Dev

ATHEISM

*A*theism is when you do not believe either in values or in the abstract. When an atheist comes to the guru, what happens? You start experiencing your own form and discover that you are indeed formless, hollow and empty. And this abstract non-form in you becomes more and more concrete.

The guru makes the abstract more real and what you thought was solid appears to be more unreal. Sensitivity and subtlety dawn. Perception of love, not as an emotion, but as the substratum of existence, becomes evident. The formless spirit shines through every form in creation and the mystery of life deepens, shattering atheism. Then the journey begins and it has four stages.

The first stage is Saarupya - to see the formless in the form - seeing God in all the forms. Often, one feels more comfortable seeing God as formless rather than with a form, because with a form, one feels a distance, a duality, a fear of rejection and other limitations. In life all of our interactions are with a form, other than in deep sleep and in samadhi. And, if you do not see God in the form, then the waking part of life remains devoid of the Divine. All those who accept God to be formless use symbols, and perhaps love the symbols more than

God himself. If God comes and tells a Christian to leave the cross or a Muslim to drop the crescent, perhaps he may not do it. To begin with, loving the formless is possible only through forms.

The second stage is Saamipya - closeness - feeling absolutely close to the form you have chosen and reaching out to the formless. This leads to a sense of intimacy with the whole creation. In this stage, one overcomes the fear of rejection and other fears. But this is bound by time and space.

The third stage is Saanidhya - feeling the presence of the Divine by which you transcend the limitations of time and space.

Then the final stage - Saayujya - is when you are firmly entrenched in the Divine. It is then you realize you are one with the Divine. There is a total merging with the Beloved and all duality disappears.

This is that and that is this.

Vinod: Does a believer also go through these four stages?

Sri Sri: Certainly, whether an atheist or believer, he goes through the four stages.

News Flash

The power of knowledge is obvious when impossible becomes possible. All arrangements for a mega event in Bangalore were made in just four days time, where Guruji and His Holiness the Dalai Lama addressed 150,000 people. His Holiness the Dalai Lama visited the ashram and addressed the Advanced Course participants and praised the Art of Living Foundation for its work towards enriching human values around the world.

The satsang was an historic moment. As Buddhist monks and Vedic pundits chanted, thousands, from the stillness of meditation, started singing, dancing and celebrating with lit candles held in their hands.

Waves of love, light and joy permeated the atmosphere. Five thousand peace balloons were sent up in the air. As the crowd pleaded for more, Guruji led them through a second round of meditation. As if this was not enough, Guruji granted everyone one wish and the next day thousands of grateful calls were received.

Youth Training Program camps are happening at many places in India.

Jai Guru Dev

To Say "Sorry" is a Good Mistake

*O*ften, in establishing your righteousness, you are insensitive to others' feelings. When someone is hurt, arguing with them and establishing your righteousness will be in vain. By simply saying "sorry," you can uplift the other person and take away the bitterness. In many situations saying "sorry" is better than establishing your righteousness - it can avert much unpleasantness.

This one word of five letters, when said sincerely, can remove anger, guilt, hatred and distance.

Many people feel pride in hearing "sorry" from others - it boosts their ego. But when you say "sorry" to a wise man, it evokes compassion at your ignorance. And when you say "sorry" to your guru, he will get angry and say, "Go! Listen to Ashtavakra!" *(laughter)* Your saying "sorry" indicates doership - you feel that YOU have MADE a mistake.

A mistake is part of an unconscious mind. An unconscious mind cannot do right, while a conscious mind can do no wrong. The mind that makes the mistake and the mind that realizes the mistake - saying "sorry" - are entirely different, aren't they? The mind that says "sorry" cannot be an unconscious mind.

Therefore, saying "sorry" sincerely is a big mistake.

Did you get it or are you confused? If you did not get it, do not feel sorry or...you can feel sorry! *(laughter)*

How strange - truth is paradoxical!

News Flash
Guruji was the chief guest at the 86th birthday celebration of Swami Satchidananda (of the Lotus Temple, Virginia) in Coimbatore. This was followed by a satsang. He also inaugurated the K.G. Eye Hospital and addressed the doctors and computer professionals.

The European Ashram was all set to welcome the master for the Christmas Advanced Course. On looking at the beautifully decorated Christmas tree, Guruji reminded everybody to be like a Christmas tree, evergreen and full of gifts. The Advanced Course at the European Ashram ended with full hearts, warm smiles and cold snow.

On to Canada for the New Year.

Jai Guru Dev

KICK THE BALL AND BE IN THE GOAL

*D*o you know why the earth is shaped like a globe?
(silence....)

So you can kick it and it will roll away! From the moment you wake up in the morning you are always with people and your mind is caught up in worldly thoughts. So sometime during the day, sit for a few minutes, get into the cave of your heart with your eyes closed and kick the world away like a ball.

But as soon as you open your eyes, hold onto the ball because you need to kick it again in the next session. *(laughter)* During the day be 100 percent attached to the work; do not try to detach yourself. But when you sit for meditation, then totally detach yourself. Only those who can totally detach can take total responsibility.

Eventually you will be able to be both attached and detached simultaneously. Kick the ball and be in the goal! This is the art of living, the skill of living.

News Flash

Two hundred and fifty people "kicked the ball" and welcomed the New Year in deep meditation with Guruji. The North American Ashram, deep in snow that sparkled like diamonds, seemed suitably decked out to receive Guruji on this first winter visit. The frozen lakes provided great "skating" on afternoon walks (runs!) through the snow.

The City Council in Alpharetta, Georgia, U.S.A., planned to remove several 150-year-old oak trees as part of a street-widening project. The engineering firm, cable company, and phone company made their studies and gave approval. Local people who wanted to save the trees were told, "There's no hope; it's finished." A devotee - Juanita Rocca - put Guruji's picture on each tree and phoned the city officials to tell them the trees were protected by a saint. Word spread through the town and 300 protestors, along with full media coverage, showed up at the City Council. Plans were abandoned, and the trees are happily standing.

Jai Guru Dev

"Important" and "Unimportant"

So many people are stuck with what is "important," always caught up in thinking about what is important. Why do you always have to do only that which is important?

For something to be important, there needs to be many things that are unimportant. So you cannot eliminate unimportant things. It is important to have unimportant things to make something else important. *(laughter)* Things are either themselves important or they make other things important. So that means everything is important, and everything is unimportant.

When you realize this fact, you become choiceless.

When you say something is important, you are limiting your vastness.

A journalist asked me, "Why is it important to breathe?" "Why is it important to be happy?" "Why is it important to have peace?" These questions are not relevant at all. Why should you always look for what is important? Something that is unimportant can contribute to something that is important. And what is important and unimportant changes with time and space. Food is important when you are hungry and unimportant when you are full.

When something is inevitable, you do not categorize it as important or unimportant. It is beyond choice.

"Everything is important" is karma yoga. "Nothing is important" is deep meditation.

∽

News Flash
Two African countries, Benin and Togo, have entered the Art of Living family - bringing the total number of countries to 112.

A Montreal devotee who is a cab driver by profession picked up a passenger one night who appeared overcome by drugs and alcohol. The passenger demanded to be taken to his destination for half-fare, and when the driver protested the passenger pulled a gun. At first the driver was afraid, but when he looked at the photo of Guruji on the dashboard he felt completely protected. During the drive the passenger put the gun away. Eventually he asked who the person was in the photo. When they reached the destination, the passenger bowed to the picture and paid the full fare to the driver along with a handsome tip.

Jai Guru Dev

WORSHIP - A SIGN OF MATURITY

*F*or a flame to rise up, you need space above it. In
the same way, for a man to rise up in his life, he needs
an ideal, he needs something to adore and worship. In
worship, a sense of belongingness, love, honor and
respect all come together. However, without a sense of
belongingness, worship or idealism can bring low self-
esteem. The ancient people knew this so they insisted
that people should feel a part of what they worship.
They encouraged people to worship the sun, moon,
mountains, rivers, plants, animals and people. Worship
is the culmination of love and appreciation. Worship
prevents love from turning into hatred or jealousy, and
prevents appreciation from becoming low self-esteem.
In life, if you do not adore or appreciate anything, you
will be filled with negativity. And a person who has
nothing to worship or adore is sure to fall into
depression.

Lack of adoration has led to many emotional,
psychological and social problems in society. If you have
nothing to hold high in life, selfishness, arrogance and
violence are sure to follow. Adoring and honoring each
other in society eliminates stress and fosters compassion
and love.

In the previous century, it was thought that worshiping was an uncivilized and unintelligent thing to do. Worship was thought to rise from a slavish mentality. In fact it is just the contrary. Worship can only happen through gratefulness and not through subservience.

Worship in a true sense is a sign of maturity and not of weakness.

Question: You said worship is the culmination of love. Does worship also have a culmination?

Sri Sri: Culmination of worship is self-knowledge, samadhi.

∽

News Flash
Guruji stopped at the European Ashram on his way to the Khumba Mela in India, where 80 million people are assembled to worship the river Ganges and Mother Nature.

Jai Guru Dev

THE KUMBHA MELA

Once every 12 years, all the seers, saints and aspirants of spiritual knowledge congregate at the confluence, or sangam, of the three holy rivers - Ganga, Yamuna and Saraswati. The Ganga is a symbol of knowledge and self-inquiry. It is on the banks of the Yamuna that events of love have been immortalized. When knowledge and love come together, when the head meets the heart, Saraswati, symbolic of wisdom and the fine arts, emerges.

When a tiny atom explodes, the radiation lasts for a long time. The mind is more subtle than one millionth of an atom. When the mind explodes, that is enlightenment.

Over the centuries, thousands of sages who have meditated, done penance and have been enlightened come to the Kumbha Mela and relieve themselves of the burden of the merits gained through Sadhana by bathing in the rivers. The water can absorb the energy that they radiate. The seekers, who come from all corners to be in the company of seers and saints, gain that merit when they take a dip in the rivers.

Space by itself cannot be bought, and a lump of clay has no value, but when space is enveloped by clay it gains value, this is a kumbha - a pot. Spirit is everywhere in nature, but when it dawns in the human body as an elevated state of consciousness, then it gains immense value. An embodied and elevated spirit is usually referred to as kumbha. This is why the enlightened age is also called the Aquarian age. Kumbha denotes a pot, which is symbolic of fullness and perfection.

The Kumbha Mela is an ancient version of a spiritual expo.

∽

News Flash
Guruji was in Prayag for the Kumbha Mela. Many very touching incidents happened that show the depth of devotion of the people who had gathered there. Here are two of them.

One morning, Guruji noticed an 80-year-old woman who had been separated from her family. She looked tired and hungry. Guruji sent someone to give her some money, which she refused to accept saying that she had come here to give, not to take! Guruji himself had to go to her and tell her that the money was prasad, which she then took from him.

It was very cold there every night, the temperature dropping to 2 or 3 degrees Celsius, and many people had no accommodations whatsoever and would just sleep in the sand on the banks of the rivers, most of them without even a shawl to cover themselves. Guruji along with some yuvacharyas and other devotees would go and distribute many blankets every night to these people. Thousands of blankets were distributed each night. One night, they came across a teenager who was shivering with cold and gave him some blankets to cover himself with, which he refused to take saying, that he could bear this cold, and that there were so many others who would need them much more.

Guruji later told everyone to note the devotion and the total surrender of these people who even in such desperate circumstances had such absolute faith in the Divine and knew that He would provide for them.

Our Ashram was bustling with activity all day long and attracted many people; food was being served continuously throughout the day. The community of saints there was overjoyed to meet with Guruji and lauded the work of the Art of Living.

Back in Delhi Guruji had very fruitful meetings with various leaders including the leader of Jamma Masjid.

Jai Guru Dev

THE OTHER SIDE OF FRIENDLINESS

Secretaries, police, judges, accountants and people in key positions should not be friendly!

The main disadvantages of being friendly are:

✦ You come under obligation.

✦ You lose your freedom.

✦ Your perception cannot be free and fair. Your thoughts and actions may not be impartial.

✦ Your focus, commitment, creativity and above all your time will be wasted.

✦ You become prone to picking up bad habits and negative moods.

It takes wisdom to be free from the burden of obligation and not be influenced by your friends' opinions and feelings.

On many occasions, it is better to be unfriendly than friendly. Being unfriendly does not mean being aggressive and inimical. The best secretaries, personal assistants, security personnel, and judges have to be unfriendly.

Those who are aloof and indifferent get centered more quickly than those who are too friendly. A certain degree of aloofness in every relationship will strengthen your personality and connect you to your source.

Vinod Sethi: It's very easy to be very aloof or very friendly. But to be friendly and aloof is a sadhana.

Harish: Be an unfriendly friend!

News Flash
From the Kumbha Mela, where he was one with even the poorest of the poor, Guruji descended on the beautiful Alpine ski resort of Davos where the richest of the rich had gathered to participate in the World Economic Forum. Guruji was invited to the World Economic Forum to participate in a dialogue with other spiritual and religious leaders from the Vatican, Israel, Egypt, Bosnia, South Africa, France and the United Kingdom.

It was a rare opportunity for the extremely busy créme de la créme of global business to interact with an even busier Guru!

Guruji was the guest of honor at a reception hosted in his honor by a leading media magnate of Europe. In his welcoming speech, the host felicitated Guruji and praised his beautiful energy. Other dignitaries who attended the reception included Shimon Peres - ex-prime minister of

Israel, Peter Gabriel - pop singer, Reinhold Messner - mountaineer, Michael Dell - CEO Dell Computers, members of the European Royalty and CEOs of Fortune 50 companies. In the jam-packed hall, Guruji was the center of attraction, as all the guests lined up to greet him personally. Several guests were heard commenting that they could feel Guruji's energy in every corner of the room!

In the concluding session of the meeting, Guruji addressed the conference and said, "Globalization was pioneered by religious and spiritual leaders long ago. Whether you like it or not, you are all our followers!"

In India, hundreds of Art of Living volunteers are busily engaged in the relief efforts in the state of Gujarat. Within hours of the earthquake, our volunteers provided shelter and food to 1,500 people. Our satsang groups are arranging food, clothing, water and funds.

Jai Guru Dev

LONGING ITSELF IS DIVINE

*L*onging itself is Divine.
Longing for worldly things makes you inert.
Longing for infinity fills you with life.

When longing dies, inertia sets in. But longing also brings along a sense of pain. To avoid the pain, you try to push away the longing. The skill is to bear the pain of longing and move on. Do not try to find a shortcut to overcome longing. Do not make the longing short - that's why it is called loooonging. *(laughter)*

True longing in itself brings up spurts of bliss. That is why in ancient days longing was kept alive by singing and listening to kathas (stories).

When longing transcends relationships, judgments, jealousy and all other negative feelings drop off. It is only with wisdom and self-knowledge that you can transcend relationships. People often think wisdom is devoid of longing - No! Such wisdom is dry. The longing that comes in true wisdom makes life juicier. Divine is certainly juicy!

Longing gives you the power to bless. Bless the entire creation. For the longing in you is God.

News Flash

Guruji's whirlwind tour of the state of Kerala, India began with hundreds of thousands celebrating at the Trivandrum satsang. At Punaloor, over 50,000 people braved heavy rains for a "standing satsang" throughout which Guruji also stood. Hundreds of thousands rejoiced at Cherokolpuzha and Kottayam satsangs.

Guruji met with His Holiness Basilius Marthoma Matthew, the second Catholic Baba, and a descendant of St. Thomas. Guruji was the chief guest at a meeting attended by Mr. George Fernandes, Defense Minister of India, and inaugurated homes for the aged at Suttur, near Mysore.

On to the Southern Kumbha Mela where he graced hundreds of thousands taking the holy dip in the water at a confluence of rivers.

The intense longing of phase 2 teacher training graduates and ashramites pulled our precious Guruji by helicopter from the Southern Kumbha Mela to reach the Bangalore Ashram just in time for a juicy satsang.

Jai Guru Dev

BACK TO SPACE

*F*rom time to time the earth shakes and in its shaking wakes up the man who is in slumber, who not only misuses Nature but puts his faith in bricks and mortar. Your true security is in the Self, not in bricks and mortar. Perhaps this is what Nature wants to convey to you. Earthquakes, floods and volcanoes all drive home the truth that nothing is permanent and you can find no security in that which is impermanent. Disasters come to you as a shock and wake you up.

When such calamities occur we try to understand their cause so that we can blame someone. Strangely, when you find someone to blame you feel comfortable, but with natural calamities you cannot blame anyone. They come to you as a shock. With wisdom, shocks can make you grow in leaps and bounds. Without wisdom a shock can only lead you to negativity and depression.

Question: Why should nature destroy small innocent children?

Sri Sri: Nature just does its job. It does not discriminate between young and old. Do you think that all those who eat bamboo shoots and eggs or pluck flower buds are not compassionate? Maybe, maybe not! *(laughter)*

Instead of questioning Nature, wake up and see the opportunity for seva or service. See what is happening in Gujarat now. Today, hundreds and thousands are engaged in service activities which would not have happened otherwise. One positive thing coming out of destruction is the reconstruction of Gujarat which would not have happened if not for the earthquake. Another interesting outcome is a fresh water spring that has appeared in a region that has been continuously drought prone.

Wisdom is considering the earth as your Valentine. Whether it shakes or breaks, it is dear to you. You always see good coming from it.

The four elements, other than space, create turbulence from time to time. If you depend on them for support, they will shake you and lead you back to space.

Finding security in inner space is spirituality.

News Flash
Guruji was a state guest in Andhra Pradesh. His talk to the government officials was greatly appreciated by the Chief Minister. Guruji was invited to come and deliver more programs in that state. That evening there was a mammoth satsang.

The Art of Living Foundation has adopted 26 villages in Kutch-Bhuj, the earthquake-hit area of Gujarat.

Twenty-five-year-old Rajani from Bangalore all of a sudden completely lost her hearing (sensorineural hearing loss) on the 9th of December, 2000. The world had become silent to her. Medical experts, after diagnosis and treatment, declared no possibility that she would regain her hearing. After attending the first day of the residential basic course at the Ashram on the 19th of January, 2001, she miraculously regained her hearing. Where medical science had failed, her Guru's grace transformed her life.

Research at the All India Institute of Medical Science showed significant changes in the brain wave patterns of the Art of Living teachers who participated in the study. All 18 subjects were found to maintain high integrity and awareness during activity.

Jai Guru Dev

PASSION AND SELF-RELIANCE

*P*assion makes you weak. Dispassion is strength.

For your passion to be fulfilled, you have to depend upon so many things. Passion and self-reliance do not appear to go together. If you are passionate, you have to forget about being self-reliant. If you want to be self-reliant, you have to drop your passion. This is generally true.

That which brings together these two completely different aspects in you is your spirit. The same spirit that wants to be self-reliant is also passionate. It is only in spirituality that passion and dispassion can happen together. This is the rarest combination.

When you are dispassionate, you have strength, and strength is self-reliance. True self-reliance is realizing that nothing is excluded from the Self. And when you realize everything is part of the Self, then you can be passionate about everything! Even to fulfill your passion, you need to only rely on the Self, for Self alone is non-changing.

In Truth, there is neither reliance nor passion. In one state, you can either be passionate or you can be self-reliant. But in an elevated state of consciousness, you can be neither, or both!

∽

News Flash
Shivratri - From every corner of India, and from all over the world, devotees came for Shiva's blessings!

Despite the Ashram overflowing with thousands, there was absolutely no chaos as the volunteers of the YTP (Youth Training Program) did wonderful seva and won everyone's hearts. It was celebration all round; even the ice creams sold like hot cakes. During the morning Rudra-puja, even the windows of the meditation hall were filled to capacity. Huge screens were laid out in the amphitheater for the evening puja, which was followed by a spellbinding satsang with Guruji truly Bholenath - Lord of the Innocent! The celebrations continued until early morning as devotees queued for darshan.

Jai Guru Dev

THE OTHER SIDE OF FEAR - THE USEFULNESS OF FEAR

*N*ature has put an amount of inbuilt fear in all living beings. This fear makes life defend itself, protect itself. Like salt in the food, a little bit of fear is essential for people to be righteous.

Fear of hurting someone makes you more conscious.
Fear of failure makes you more keen and dynamic.
Fear moves you from carelessness to taking care.
Fear moves you from insensitivity to sensitivity.
Fear moves you from dullness to alertness.

Total lack of fear may lead to destructive tendencies - a distorted ego knows no fear. Neither does one with expanded consciousness! Whereas the ego dismisses fear and moves in a destructive manner, the wise one acknowledges fear and takes refuge in the Divine.

When you are in love, when you are surrendered, there is no fear. Ego, too, knows no fear. But there is a difference, like that of heaven and earth, between these two types of fearless states.

Fear makes you righteous; fear brings you close to surrender; fear keeps you on the path; fear keeps you from being destructive. Peace and law are maintained on the planet because of fear.

A newborn child knows no fear - it totally relies on its mother. Whether a child, a kitten or a bird, when they start becoming independent they experience fear which makes them go running back to their mothers. This is inbuilt by nature to sustain life.

So, the purpose of fear is to bring you back to the source!

News Flash
Guruji's entire journey from Mumbai to Surat was punctuated by darshan. Enthusiastic devotees, in hundreds, thronged every station. 40,000 attended the live Kriya in Surat setting off a wave of energy, culminating in a 'high-voltage' satsang of over 300,000 people.

On to Ahmedabad, where Guruji's meeting with the Chief Minister and bureaucrats proved extremely useful. Guruji suggested drastic changes in the layout plan of the 900 quake-hit villages which are to be rebuilt. His ideas were greatly appreciated and immediately incorporated.

Guruji wondered whether he was awakening people or not, but devotees who showed up all night at different stations between Ahmedabad and Udaipur, armed with musical bands, definitely kept waking up everyone with their fervor!

Guruji's first ever visit to the city of Jheels (lakes), Udaipur, saw a grand satsang. He also met with other NGOs and gave a highly illuminating talk on Integrated Social Development. Gliding softly over the moonlit waters in a boat to the glittering Jagmandir, he was given a royal reception and the satsang happened in regal splendor!

"When the Divine dwells in your heart, the whole world appears to you as a temple."

Guruji's entourage decided that it was high time he stopped traveling by train. On the last leg of this wonderfully eventful trip from Udaipur to Delhi, there was a brief stop-over for 20 minutes at Jaipur where a welcome stage and over a thousand devotees compelled Guruji to deplane and give darshan right there, even at the airport, where satsang happened spontaneously!

Jai Guru Dev

THE OTHER SIDE OF EGO

*E*go is an impediment for a leader, a wise man, a merchant or a servant, but it is a necessity for a warrior, a competitor. A warrior is one who takes on challenges and commitments and stands by them.

Ego makes one sacrifice oneself for a cause. Ego gives strength and courage, brings valor to meet the challenges with endurance and perseverance. A strong ego will counteract depression. Often ego is thought to be selfish but it is the greatest motivating factor for creativity and generosity.

Ego propels one to venture into the unknown.

There are three types of ego - sattvic, rajasic and tamasic.

◆ Tamasic ego is barbaric and blind, and has self-destructive tendencies.

◆ Rajasic ego is self-centered and causes misery to oneself and others.

◆ Sattvic ego is creative and has protective tendencies.

If you cannot surrender, at least have a sattvic ego, as a sattvic ego is always ready to sacrifice.

Bhanu: This is very good! It gives many people relief. *(laughter)*

∽

News Flash
Rishikesh camp begins with the first Advanced Course where joy and silence go hand in hand. Knowledge is flowing like the Ganges.

So far, 50 truckloads of materials have reached the areas severely hit by the earthquake in Gujarat. Our teachers are busy having courses to help people deal with their trauma.

Jai Guru Dev

THE PARADOX OF SACRIFICE

All the scriptures of the world glorify sacrifice. What is sacrifice?

It is giving up something that you value. You can only sacrifice that which you would like to keep for yourself; in other words, that which gives you pleasure and joy. You cannot sacrifice something that you dislike or disown. Sacrifice is always related to a higher cause for a greater good. At the same time, when your love for the greater good is so strong, nothing else assumes any value. Sacrifice here becomes irrelevant, because love alone is your strongest driving force. So when there is so much love there cannot be sacrifice. At the same time when there is no love, there is no sacrifice.

For example, if a mother has made plans to see a movie and she realizes that her child is sick, she does not say that she has sacrificed the movie to nurse her child, because she simply did not want to go. Nothing else seems to charm the mother besides being with her child.

You do not sacrifice something for someone you are in love with. Sacrifice indicates that your pleasure has more value than the cause for which you are sacrificing.

When the love is lukewarm, then sacrifice assumes meaning. Yet sacrifice purifies the human mind and reins in selfish tendencies. It can also bring pride, arrogance, self-pity and sometimes even depression.

You can sacrifice only that which you value. For a wise man nothing is more valuable than truth, values and the Divine, and he will never sacrifice those. God is the greatest, and if someone values the greatest, then how can he sacrifice God? This is the paradox of sacrifice.

News Flash
Holi celebrations were simply memorable. With colors in the air, the celebrations transported people back in time on the banks of the Ganga.

Thousands got together in 43 cities all over the world to participate in the 5H Walk for Gujarat to rehabilitate the earthquake-destroyed areas of Gujarat, India. It was well covered by the media.

Pakistan is the latest addition to the list of countries where Art of Living Courses are conducted, bringing the total to 113.

Jai Guru Dev

DIVINE IN THE FORM AND FORMLESS

*D*ivinity is unmanifest, but man has an innate desire to perceive the Divine in the manifest creation around him. He creates idols, breathes faith into them and requests divinity to be present in the idol for a while, so that he can worship, express his love and play with it. At the end of his worship he requests divinity to go back into his heart from where divinity manifested. This is in all puja practices.

Participants in the puja are not actually worshipping the idols but are worshipping the unmanifest divinity which has the divine qualities. So, the idol worshippers of the East are not the same as the ones in the Middle East described in the Bible, because they are not just worshipping different gods and different idols, they are worshipping the ONE divinity in many different forms.

Paganism, Satan and animal worship, without the knowledge of the one divinity is very different from seeing the Divine in every form of the manifest universe. In the eastern tradition, gods and goddesses are part of the one divinity like the different colors of white sunlight, whereas in the Greek tradition, gods and goddesses are in themselves different entities.

Worshipping Satan and different entities is totally
different from worshipping divinity in its various forms.
Every form belongs to the Divine. When you adore the
form, you are adoring the Divine behind the form.

With this knowledge, the very act of worship, which is
more an inner phenomenon, assumes a more colorful
and vibrant expression, indicating that both the form
and the formless are all divine.

∞

News Flash
*Guruji dashed to Delhi for a brief 48-hour visit where he
rapped with the law students telling them that LAW stood
for Love, Awareness and Wisdom. Human Resources stands
both for Heart and Rational thinking, he emphasized
while inaugurating an H.R. portal, and later converted a
group of eminent scientists at the National Physical
Laboratory to having both a scientific and spiritual temper
by saying, "All discoveries are a product of consciousness."
Provoking the leaders of business at the Associated
Chambers of Commerce and Industry, he said, "If God can
play man, why should man not play God?"*

*Ten schools have been opened in northeastern India and
eleven school buildings are under construction in Gujarat.*

Jai Guru Dev

STRENGTH AND SUBORDINATION

*M*any people do not want to work under someone else, be it in their profession, a company or even voluntary service. The general notion is that when you work under someone, you lose your freedom, you have to be answerable.

So, many people opt for business, wanting to be their own boss. But, in business, you are accountable to so many people. If you cannot be accountable to even one person, how can you be accountable to many? This is the paradox. In fact, being in business binds you more than the boss!

Refusing to work under someone is a sign of weakness, not strength. A strong person would not feel uncomfortable working under anyone, because he knows his strength. It is the weak and poor in spirit who do not like to work under someone else, because they are unaware of their strength. They can be neither successful in business nor in any profession.

And the same is true even in the field of social service - often volunteers do not want to work under someone else. This is merely an exhibition of their weakness. With such an attitude, they achieve very little.

One who is timid and weak in spirit would be uncomfortable to work even under the wise one; but one who knows his own strength can work effectively even under a fool!

Nityanand: But to work under a fool is frustrating!

Sri Sri: When you know your strength, with skill and intelligence, you can turn every disadvantage into an advantage. A fool can bring out the best of your communication skills! *(laughter)*

So watch out! If you feel uncomfortable working under someone, it clearly shows you need to strengthen yourself. Desiring freedom from circumstances, situations or people is no freedom at all. Knowing that nobody can take away your freedom - that is strength! And when you realize your strength is unshakable, you will not mind working under anybody.

~

News Flash
Over a thousand people took part in a 5H Walk at Muscat, in which the Royal family also participated.

Dehradun had a scintillating satsang. The Advanced Course in Rishikesh had knowledge, bliss and grace! The Hindu New Year was heralded with an early morning dip in the holy Ganges by Guruji and all the devotees.

Jai Guru Dev

COMMITMENT AND CONVENIENCE

A commitment can only be felt when it oversteps convenience. That which is convenient is not commitment. If you just go on your convenience, your commitment falls apart causing more inconvenience! If you keep dropping your commitment because it is inconvenient, can you be comfortable? Often, what is convenient does not bring comfort, but gives an illusion of comfort. Also if you are too stuck in commitment, and it is too inconvenient too often, you will be unable to fulfill your commitment and it will only generate frustration. Wisdom is to strike a balance between convenience and commitment because both bring comfort to the body, mind and spirit.

A seeker of knowledge should forget about convenience, so should soldiers, rulers, students, seekers of wealth and all essential service providers. Those who want to be creative and adventurous transcend convenience. Those who are ambitious and have a passion for a goal do not care for convenience. To the wise their commitment is their comfort. Whenever their commitment is shaken, their comfort is also shaken. To the lazy, commitment is torture though it is the best remedy.

Commitment will always bring comfort in the long run.

Question: Are there any commitments that can be given up?

Sri Sri: Yes. Sometimes when you are committed without a vision, you feel stifled when your vision expands. Such commitments made with shortsightedness can be given up.

◆ A smaller less important commitment can be given up for a greater commitment.

◆ Commitment to the means can be given up for the sake of the commitment to the goals.

◆ When your commitment brings misery to many in the long run, it can be given up.

Knowledge splash!
Guruji held up a pistachio nut and asked, "What is this?"

Everybody said, "Pistachio."

Guruji held up a pistachio nut without the shell and asked, "What is this?"

Everybody said, "Pistachio."

Guruji then held up the shell and asked, "What is this?"

Everybody said, "Shell."

Guruji then said, "As the nut with or without the shell is 'pistachio', similarly spirit with or without the body is God. But just as the shell without the nut is not pistachio, the body without spirit is not God. Spirit is certainly God because it is present everywhere. The body is certainly not God because it cannot be present everywhere."

When someone asks you, "Are you God?" - who is the question addressed to? As it is only the spirit that answers, you have no choice but to say, "Yes!"

When asked, "Are you God?"- the best answer is: God is within the body and God embodies the whole universe. Those who have eyes will see.

Jai Guru Dev

DEALING WITH BLAME AND ACCUSATION

When someone blames you, you feel a heavy load on your head, and when you talk about it you spread the unpleasant feeling all around you. At that moment wake up and see you are Being and nothing can touch you. This is all just a drama that you yourself have created. You have gone through this over and over again. All the accusations you face in your life are your own creation. Knowing this, you feel free and light.

Owning responsibility for all your experiences in life makes you powerful and will put an end to grumbling, planning counterattacks, explanations, and a host of negative tendencies. Owning full responsibility makes you free.

When someone blames you, directly or indirectly, what do you do?

✦ Do you lodge it in your mind and get emotionally upset?

✦ Do you dismiss it and the blamer altogether without taking a lesson from it?

✦ Do you talk about it with people and waste your time and other's time and money?

✦ Do you pity yourself and blame your shortcomings?

+ Do you blame the other person?

+ Do you generalize and eternalize the problem?

When this happens you are not living up to the knowledge. You need to do the basic course at least half a dozen times and read all the weekly knowledge.

+ Do you laugh at it and not even take notice of it?

+ Do you treat it as a non-event, not even worth talking about, let alone taking any action?

+ Do you treat comments and accusations as passing clouds and more of an entertainment?

+ Do you discourage dwelling on unpleasant and negative moments?

+ Do you remain nonjudgmental and absolutely unshaken in your space of love?

+ Outwardly you may be calm, but do you also remain centered and calm within you, not even taking pride in your growth or wisdom?

Then you are a pride to your tutor - the master.

You cannot take credit for loving Guruji or any wise person. You have no choice at all as it will happen against all odds!

To love someone whom you like is not a big deal at all.

To love someone because they love you, gets you zero marks.

To love someone whom you do not like, means you have learned a lesson in life.

To love someone who blames you for no reason, shows you have learned the art of living.

News Flash
A gentleman complained to Guruji that some people have ganged up against him and blamed him. Guruji patiently listened, adding a few comments. The person felt he gained some sympathy and as he started feeling righteous, Guruji shot back saying, "You have already wasted enough of your time. Why do you want to waste mine also! You only get what you have sown!" Suddenly the whole atmosphere became serene and smiles returned.

Jai Guru Dev

SELF-CONFIDENCE AND AMBITION

*A*mbition indicates a lack of self-confidence!

When you know you can achieve something easily, you are not ambitious about it. You are simply confident that you can do it. Your ambition indicates challenge and uncertainty, which is contrary to self-confidence. So one who has total self-confidence cannot be ambitious! At the same time a person who lacks total self-confidence cannot be ambitious either! For ambition to be, one must have a little bit of confidence and total ignorance of the Self.

It is next to impossible to have total confidence without Self-knowledge. With the knowledge of the Self, there is nothing left to achieve, for the entire nature of existence is mere play and display of one's own consciousness.

People take pride in being ambitious. The wise man will only smile at them. Ambition can never be for something you know you can achieve effortlessly. You can only be ambitious about something for which you must put forth effort, which poses a challenge and which you are not even certain you will be able to achieve.

Moreover, ambition takes away the joy of the moment.

With Self-knowledge nothing is challenging to you, nor do you need to exert any effort. Nature is ready to fulfill your intentions even before they arise, giving you no chance to crave or desire. Nature does not allow the wise to have desires or ambitions, nor does it allow the unwise to fulfill or get rid of them.

Do you still want to be ambitious or is your only ambition to get rid of ambition? *(laughter)*

News Flash
After a fantastic satsang in Los Angeles, and a brief stopover in Apple Valley, California, Guruji left for his Central and South American tour.

Guruji is encouraging satsang groups to read the Yoga Vasistha.

Jai Guru Dev

THE DANGERS OF BELONGINGNESS AND ADVANTAGES OF OBLIGATIONS

*B*elongingness can bring about a host of negative emotions like demand, jealousy, unawareness and lack of gratitude. Just look into your own life - you feel more grateful to strangers than the people you feel "belong" to you. Belongingness reduces gratefulness, awareness, and gives rise to demands which destroy love. This is the biggest problem in relationships. People are nice to strangers and give more attention to them but with a sense of belongingness comes a lack of attention and a sense of being carefree.

Belongingness can make you insensitive, dull, and take away the charm in life. Who belongs to whom in this world? Here you are a stranger and everyone is a stranger to you. Blessed are those who feel themselves a stranger.

You feel more obligation to a stranger than to the person you feel belongs to you. Obligation is very good for keeping a check on your ego. It makes you humble. There is no greater antidote to ego than humility. Being humble is the beginning of all virtues.

People have such resistance to obligations. They do not realize that they are always under obligation, whether giving or taking. Dull people think that one is obliged only when one takes. The wise know that even when giving, one is under obligations as the person has accepted what one gives. So whether you give or take you are under obligations. And if someone does not give or take, you are still under obligation, for they are freeing you from visible obligations. That is to say, you are obliged even to those who do not make you obliged.

Life renews itself constantly by becoming a stranger in this old and familiar world. You are simply loaded with obligations and you are a total stranger in this world every moment. How does it feel?

News Flash
In Suriname, the Vice-President, Speaker of the Parliament and other parliamentarians received Guruji, and later the Army, Navy, Air Force, and the prison and police chiefs met with Guruji. They were greatly impressed with the Art of Living programs and requested that they be offered continuously.

Guruji was received at the chamber of the Vice-Governor of Bahia, Brazil. As Guruji entered a great sense of calmness dawned on everyone. The Vice-President shared that there was a conflict going on over border issues, and suddenly within moments of Guruji's arrival in the building, it was resolved.

At the Recife Airport, Guruji played tricks on all those who were accompanying him, so everyone said they would not listen to him anymore.

Jai Guru Dev

PRESTIGE AND HONOR - YOUR GOLDEN CAGE

*H*onor reduces freedom. Your fame, honor and virtue can limit your freedom.

Nobody expects a good person to make a mistake. So the better you are, the higher the expectations people have of you. It is then that you lose your freedom. Your virtues and good actions are like a golden cage. You are trapped by your own good actions, for everyone expects more from a good person and nobody expects anything from a bad person.

Most of the people are stuck in this cage of prestige and honor. They cannot smile. They are constantly worried about keeping up their prestige and their honor. It becomes more important than their own life. Just being good or doing good to retain prestige and honor is worthless. Prestige and honor can bring more misery in life than poverty.

Many desire fame but little do they know that they are looking for a cage.

It is an art to be dignified and yet not be suffocated by it. Only the wise would know this. For the wise one it is natural to be honored, but he has no concerns even if it falls apart. Despite having fame or prestige, he will live as though he has none. A wise person can handle any fame without feeling suffocated for he too is crazy!

By doing good in society one gains prestige, then when enjoying the prestige and honor one's freedom is lost.

Question: Then how do you keep your freedom?

Sri Sri: By being like a child, considering the world as a dream, a burden or a joke.

∞

News Flash
The state assembly of Sao Paulo honored Guruji where he spoke and conducted a meditation. After a moving satsang that evening, Guruji left for Buenos Aires. In Argentina, Guruji addressed the prestigious International Counsel for Cultural Relationships and then moved on to Panama, where he addressed a group of women government and business leaders and had private meetings with the mayor, the provincial governor and the Vice President. In the evening a huge satsang was held at the local university. When the local driver got lost in Buenos Aires, Guruji magically navigated the car to find one of the 7 by 3 meter billboards with Guruji's picture.

Jai Guru Dev

Life is a Dream, a Burden or a Joke

*O*ften when you are happy you feel life is a dream because you do not believe in the reality of it. When there is misery, you feel life is a burden, and we take trivial things very seriously. But one who has really gone through the pleasure realizes that pleasure is also a burden. If you have undergone misery thoroughly you will realize that life is a dream. You have been walked or carried through every miserable condition and then you realize life is a dream. Only when you see life as a dream, a burden or a joke can you be centered.

When you have really gone through misery then you have really seen life is a dream, and in between the pain and pleasure life is all a joke.

Life is very uncertain. Before it takes you away, realize it is a dream, a burden or a joke.

Question: What about life is a joke?

Sri Sri: You do not question a joke. If you question a joke, it is no longer a joke. Do not question burden either; it is a waste of time to question life and its events.

Burden makes you go deep. It gets you to the core of yourself. Realization of a dream wakes you up and seeing life as a joke makes you light.

The only certainty is that life is a dream, a burden or a joke and only when you realize this can you be centered.

News Flash
Two of our dearest devotees, Nandita Judge and Nityanand Trehan who lived knowledge so deeply like Jenaka returned back to the source this week. They were seva warriors. They had filled the Art of Living family with love and laughter and in their departure they have deepened our dispassion and strengthened our commitment. This year the 13th of May will be a worldwide celebration and satsang honoring Nityanand and Nandita.

Jai Guru Dev

REASON AND FAITH

*R*eason is reeling in the known. Faith is moving in the unknown.

Reason is repetition. Faith is exploration.

Reason is routine. Faith is adventure.

Reason and faith are completely opposite, yet they are an integral part of life.

Not having faith itself is misery; faith gives instant comfort. While reasoning keeps you sane and grounded, miracles cannot happen without faith. Faith takes you beyond limitations. In faith you can transcend the laws of nature but your faith must be pure.

Faith is beyond reason, yet you need to have faith in your own reasoning! Faith and reason cannot exist without each other. Every reason is based on some faith. Whenever reason or faith break, confusion and chaos prevail which is often a step for growth.

There are two types of faith: faith out of fear, greed and insecurity; and faith born out of love like the faith between the mother and child, the master and disciple. Whereas faith out of love cannot be broken, faith out of fear and greed is shaky.

An atheist bases himself on reason and a believer on faith. A believer uses God as an insurance policy; he thinks he is special. In the eyes of God there is no "mine" and "others" - all are the same. An atheist rationalizes to keep his eyes shut to reality. Death shakes them both. When someone close dies, an atheist's eyes are opened and a believer's faith cracks. Only a Yogi - a wise one - remains unshaken, for that person has transcended both reason and faith.

You need a balance between faith and reason.

News Flash
On Guruji's birthday, in a grand sea of memorial services throughout the globe, the world paid moving tributes to Guruji's most beloved devotees, Nityanand and Nandita. Nityanand's parents cut the cake in Delhi, and thousands gathered in satsang, soaked in knowledge, dancing and celebrating life as well as death.

The Canadian Ashram teacher's refresher course left the teachers astounded.

Jai Guru Dev

DOING TRIVIAL THINGS

What can you do for eternity? Definitely not anything that is big or great because it needs effort and effort tires you. So, doing something great is a temporary state. If you can think of one thing that is well below your capacity to do and agree to do it for eternity, that becomes puja.

The readiness to consciously do trivial things for eternity unites you with eternity. This is an antidote to ego. Ego is always ambitious and wants to do the toughest job like climbing Mount Everest. But a simple act like watching a butterfly, watering the garden, watching the birds or the sky can bring deep relaxation; and relaxation connects you with your source. Not that you should do trivial things all your life, but consciously agreeing to do the trivial actions for eternity opens a new dimension and brings immense peace and restfulness.

To find rest in activity, choose an activity that is far below your capacity and agree to do it for all eternity. Doing a job far below your capacity and being satisfied with it will make it possible to do a job much beyond your capacity.

Know that all actions are born out of infinity and that which is born out of infinity can take you to infinity.

∽

News Flash
A traditional South Indian welcome with Poorna Kumbha, garlands and the Vaadyam greeted Guruji when he arrived at the Kodai Road station on the way to the South Zone Teacher's Meet at picturesque Kodaikanal. Devotees from the nearby areas thronged the platform, and the satsang and celebration lasted for half an hour.

The entourage then proceeded to "The Nest" at Kodaikanal which was booked exclusively for the Art of Living Teacher's Meet. Nearly 160 teachers took part in this meet and had the privilege of having Guruji exclusively to themselves for three days. They spent quality time with Guruji and had uplifting knowledge sessions with the master. Interactive discussions among the teachers kept the meet lively.

Guruji, with a few teachers, proceeded to Trichy where a satsang had been arranged.

Jai Guru Dev

JOY AND SORROW

The inability to experience joy and sorrow is inertia. Experiencing joy and sorrow is a trait of consciousness.

Being happy in one's own joy and sad in one's own sorrow is a trait of animals. Being happy at another's joy and saddened by another's sorrow is a trait of humans.

If you are saddened by others' sorrow, then sorrow will never come to you. If you are happy at another's joy, then joy will never leave you.

Seeing that every relative joy is also a misery is a sign of dispassion. Seeing both joy and sorrow as just a technique is a sign of the wise.

Considering sorrow as mere illusion is divinity. Transcending joy and sorrow and being established in the self is perfection.

As the late Swami Sharanananda said, "Pray for the strength to serve in joy and to sacrifice in sorrow."

News Flash
King Dasharatha had done the Nav Chetana Shibir (the Breath-Water-Sound Program) but Lord Rama had not taken the Art of Living Course! For clues read Yoga Vasistha.

Jai Guru Dev

DEEP REST AND BLISS

*D*eep rest is bliss and bliss is the understanding that only God exists. Knowing that only God exists is the deepest rest possible.

This conviction or experience that "only God exists" is samadhi. Samadhi is the mother of all talents, strengths and virtues. Samadhi is needed even for the most materialistic person because a materialistic person looks to gain strength and virtues. To be in samadhi you do not need any effort or talents, strengths or virtues.

Withdrawing from all types of physical and mental activity is rest. That is built into our system as sleep, and sleep is the best friend of activity.

Samadhi is a conscious rest. Samadhi is the best friend of life. To be alive in your full potential, samadhi is indispensable.

What obstructs samadhi is restlessness. How many types of restlessness are there and what are the remedies? *(The answer next week.)*

News Flash
The satsang wave moved on with Guruji from Bangalore
to Bombay to Germany. In Baden Baden, Germany,
Guruji was the keynote speaker at the Rainbow Spirit
Festival. Then on to a boat ride satsang in Paris, and a
moving satsang in Lyon. Guruji is now in Berlin.

The Art of Living Course has now been held in 132
countries. Last week the course was held in Jordan.

Jai Guru Dev

FIVE TYPES OF RESTLESSNESS

*T*here are five types of restlessness.

The first type of restlessness is due to the place you are in. When you move away from that place, the street or the house, you immediately feel better. Chanting, singing, children playing and laughing can change this atmospheric restlessness. If you chant and sing, the vibration in the place changes.

The second type of restlessness is in the body. Eating the wrong food or vata-aggravating food, eating at odd times, not exercising, and overworking can all cause a physical restlessness. The remedy for this is exercise, moderation in work habits and going on a vegetable or juice diet for one or two days.

The third type of restlessness is mental restlessness. It is caused by ambition, strong thoughts, likes or dislikes. Knowledge alone can cure this restlessness: seeing life from a broader perspective, knowing the Self and realizing the impermanence of everything. If you achieve everything, so what? After your achievement, you will die. Knowledge of your death or life, confidence in the Self, in the Divine, can all calm down this mental restlessness.

Then there is emotional restlessness. Any amount of knowledge does not help here. Only Kriya helps. All the emotional restlessness vanishes after practicing Kriya. The presence of your guru, a wise person, or a saint will also help to calm your emotional restlessness.

The fifth type of restlessness is rare. It is the restlessness of the soul. When everything feels empty and meaningless, know you are very fortunate. That longing and restlessness is the restlessness of the soul. Do not try to get rid of it. Embrace it! Welcome it! Usually to get rid of it people do all sorts of things - change places, jobs or partners, do this, do that. It seems to help for some time, but it does not last.

This restlessness of the soul alone can bring authentic prayer in you. It brings perfection, Siddhis and miracles in life. It is so precious to get that innermost longing for the Divine. Satsang and the presence of an enlightened one soothes the restlessness of the soul.

⌇

News Flash

After a memorial satsang in the biggest cathedral in Berlin, Guruji moved on to London. In Westminster Abbey and the town hall of Brent Town, satsangs exploded with enthusiastic devotees. Guruji inaugurated our new center in London. Excellent teamwork marked Guruji's much awaited London tour.

On the 13th he arrived in Strasbourg to deliver a talk at the European Parliament. It was presided by Reinholt Messner, the famous mountaineer and Peter von Kohl, the President of the Organization of Journalists of the European Parliament.

Guruji is now in the European Ashram and on Friday he will address the biggest ever gathering of Christians in Germany.

Jai Guru Dev

TENDENCIES AND INFLUENCES

*L*ife moves by dual factors: inner tendencies and outer influences.

Inner tendencies form your attitudes and behavior, while external influences make strong impressions in your mind. Often your tendencies generate external situations, and situations around you can form tendencies within you. This is what is called karma.

Both these factors - the tendencies from within and influences from outside - can be either beneficial or harmful.

It is awareness that filters the outer negative influences and it is awareness that corrects and annihilates the unhealthy inner tendencies. This awareness is called gyana. The purpose of education is to develop this awareness so that you can be selective about your tendencies and influences.

It is practically impossible to resist the external influences and the inner tendencies without raising one's consciousness. This can be gradual or sudden. And that is how a human being has both free will and destiny.

Freedom is when you have a say about your tendencies and your influences. Only awareness and impeccable devotion can bring this freedom.

⟳

News Flash
Guruji's address to the Protestant Christian Congregation in Germany was simply brilliant. Denmark, Sweden and Norway had enthralling satsangs. He is moving on to the Advanced Course in Gotenborg.

Jai Guru Dev

AUTHENTICITY AND SKILLFULNESS

Authenticity and skillfulness appear to be contradictory, but in fact they are complementary. Your intentions need to be authentic and your actions need to be skillful. The more authentic the intention, the more skillful the action will be. Authentic intention and skillful action make you unshakable.

Skill is required only when authenticity cannot have its way. Yet skill without authenticity makes you shallow. You cannot have an authentic action and a skillful intention. If you try to be authentic in your action but manipulative in your mind, that is when mistakes happen.

John: Is it possible to have a powerful intention, like greed, that is authentic?

Sri Sri: If your intention is colored by such things as greed or over-ambition, then your intention is not authentic. Whenever your intentions are impure, it pricks your consciousness, so it cannot be authentic. Authentic intentions are free from negative emotions. An action that is not skillful leads to negative emotions and an intention that is not authentic harbors negative emotions.

Gayatri: If our intention is authentic and yet our actions are not skillful, what should we do?

Sri Sri: Carry a handkerchief. *(laughter)*

Question: What is the best skill to deal with intention?

Sri Sri: Do not keep any sankalpas, or intentions, to yourself. Offer them to the Divine.

Actions can never be perfect but our intentions can be perfect. Actions always have room for improvement. Action means growth and movement, and that needs space.

The depth in you and the freedom in you bring out the skillfulness in you. Krishna was the most skillful because his silence was so deep.

News Flash
Guruji arrived in the U.S. after a wonderful Advanced
Course in Scandinavia. At the airport he set off the security
alarms to the amazement and delight of the security staff.

The Mayor of Franklin Township, New Jersey declared
June 24, to be "Ravi Shankar Day" in honor of our
founder's achievements. After grand satsangs in Raleigh,
North Carolina and Richmond, Virginia, Guruji ended
the East Coast portion of his tour at the historic
Constitution Hall on the National Mall in Washington,
D.C., just one block from the White House. The mayor of
Washington, D.C. declared June 27 as the "Art of Living
Day" in our nation's capital.

Jai Guru Dev

TIME, SPACE AND MIND

*B*ecome God to each other. Do not look for God somewhere in the sky, but see God in every pair of eyes, in the mountains, water, trees and animals. How? Only when you see God in yourself will this happen. Only Gods can worship Gods. To recognize divinity, there are three dimensions: time, space and mind.

For a seeker, it is necessary to honor time and space so he or she can experience sacredness in his or her mind. When you honor time and space, your mind becomes alert. But for the one who has transcended the mind, either sacredness has no meaning, or all time, every place and every mood is sacred.

Precious moments are few in life. Catch them and treasure them. Place, time and the mood of your mind are factors that influence celebration.

Snatch every opportunity to celebrate; then you will feel great and full. Then celebration infiltrates your mind in all moods and space, and celebration is inevitable.

Celebration reminds you of the fullness of the moment. The moments you are in the company of knowledge - the master - are the most precious moments in your life.

Treasure them. In treasuring them you transcend the mind, time and space, and that is true celebration.

∞

News Flash
Guru Purnima was celebrated surrounded by the majestic mountains and magnificent skies of Lake Tahoe. All heads were crowned by our beloved Guruji in the presence of eight Swamis of various mutts from India, the world's foremost Ayurvedic physician, Dr. Trigunaji, and Dr. Trigunaji's son.

Weeklong seva activities and slum cleanup projects were begun in Bangalore. Medical camps were set up, and clothes and food were distributed from many Art of Living centers.

While compiling this weekly knowledge, Marcy lost her mind in time and space.

Jai Guru Dev

The Art of Living Foundation

The *Art of Living Foundation* (www.artofliving.org) is devoted to making your life a celebration. A nonprofit educational organization run by volunteers, we offer workshops for self-development and spiritual growth that allow busy people to take maximum advantage of Sri Sri's multidimensional teachings. We are officially accredited as a Non-Governmental Organization (NGO) with the United Nations, and we sponsor service projects worldwide, including programs for people living with HIV and cancer, rehabilitative training for prisoners and vocational training for rural people in Asia.

Our *Care for Children "Dollar-a-Day"* program (www.careforchildren.org) provides children with food, clothing and school. Founded in 1981 and accredited as a charitable non-profit institution, *Ved Vignan Mahavidyapeeth* (Institute of Vedic Science) provides many essential educational and medical services. The only school of its kind in the area, the Institute has grown to house and serve boys and girls from 22 surrounding villages. All services are administered at no charge to each child through funding from supporting individuals and groups.

The *5-H Program* is a joint effort of the *International Association of Human Values (IAHV -* www.IAHV.org*)* and the Art of Living in India. The 5-H Program offers social and community development projects with a focus on Health, Hygiene, Homes, Harmony in Diversity, and Human Values. This unique and comprehensive approach involves training at-risk youth to become community leaders. IAHV's *Homes for Change* program is building homes, wells, and septic systems for poor families in India.

∽

The *Art of Living Course* is the ideal introduction to Sri Sri's wisdom. This 16-18 hour program over 6 days has uplifted the lives of thousands. Breath contains the secret of life. The breath links us to vital life energy, or prana. Low prana causes depression, lethargy, dullness and poor enthusiasm. When your mind and body are charged with prana, you feel alert, energetic and happy. Specific breathing techniques taught on the course revitalize and invigorate your physical and emotional well-being. Among these techniques is Sudarshan Kriya which is a powerful and unique process that fully oxygenates the cells, recharging them with new energy and life, washing away negative emotions stored as toxins in the body. Tension, anger, anxiety, depression and lethargy are released and forgotten. The mind is left calm and centered, with a clearer vision of the world, our relationships and ourselves. The course also includes processes and deep insights into the nature of life and how to be happy. To take the course contact the Art of Living Center nearest you which is listed in the directory on page 117.

Advanced Courses are specially designed for those who have completed the introductory Art of Living Course. These retreats spent in silence provide you a profound opportunity to explore the depths of your own inner silence through deep meditation, seva and enjoyable processes. Each evening ends with a celebration of singing, dancing and astounding wisdom. You leave feeling renewed emotionally and elevated spiritually, with a dynamism for greater success in all your activities. Some Advanced Courses are offered in Sri Sri's presence - personally meeting him is the experience of a lifetime.

Sahaj Samadhi Meditation. Not one of us lacks spiritual depth. The peace and happiness we feverishly seek in the world are already contained within us, but masked by stress and strain. These are released with Sahaj Samadhi meditation - another gift of tremendous value from Sri Sri. Sahaj Samadhi meditation provides a rest much deeper than sleep. Like awakening renewed on a sunny morning, your outlook on life becomes more positive. Stress drops off, the chattering mind becomes serene and creative, aging slows and you rediscover the unshakable contentment of your inner Self. Sahaj Samadhi meditation is easy to learn and practice. With simple guidance, anyone can meditate. Personal instruction is offered at Art of Living Centers worldwide.

Our courses for children and teens, the *ART Excel* Course, All 'Round Training In Excellence, provides practical techniques that enable young people to handle negative emotions such as fear, anger and frustration in positive ways. The ART Excel Course also teaches vital non-academic skills such as the art of making friends, the secret of popularity, and the value of service to others - all in a supportive, yet challenging and fun atmosphere. Our toughest critics - the kids themselves - give this program rave reviews.

∞

You can visit our web site at www.artofliving.org to learn the latest about these programs.

Art of Living Bookstore

Books, videotapes and audiotapes of Sri Sri are available by mail. Titles include: God Loves Fun, The Path of Love, Compassion and Trust, The Purpose of Life, The Ultimate Relationship, Om Shanti Shanti Shanti and the Yoga Sutras of Patanjali.

For a catalog of products and to order, contact:

Art of Living Bookstore
(877) 477-4774 U.S.A. or (641) 472-9892
Facsimile: (641) 472-0671
E-mail: bookstore@artofliving.org

Worldwide Art of Living Centers

For more information about Art of Living courses and programs, contact a center closest to you:

AFRICA
Hema & Rajaraman
Art of Living
P.O. Box 1213
Peba Close Plot 5612
Gaborone, Botswana
Tel. 26-735-2175
Aolbot@global.co.za

CANADA
Art of Living Foundation
P.O. Box 170
13 Infinity Rd.
Saint-Mathieu-du-Parc
Quebec G0X 1N0
Canada
Tel. (819) 532-3328
artofliving.northamerica@
sympatico.ca

GERMANY
Akademie Bad Antogast
Bad Antogast 1
77728 Oppenau
Germany
Tel. 49-7804-910-923
Artofliving.Germany@
t-online.de

INDIA
Vyakti Vikas Kendra, India
No. 19, 39th A Cross,
11th Main
4th T Block, Jayanagar
Bangalore 560041, India
Tel. 91-80-6645106
vvm@vsnl.com

UNITED STATES
Art of Living Foundation
P.O. Box 50003
Santa Barbara, CA 93150
Tel. 805-564-1002
U.S. toll free: 877-399-1008
info@artofliving.org